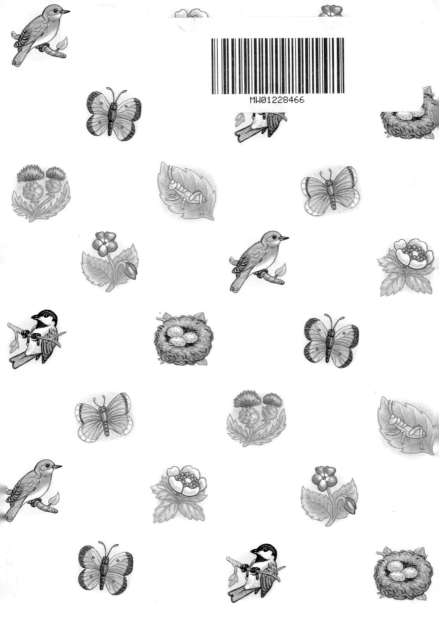

MW01228466

This book belongs to

_____

Classic Poems
for
Children

EDITED BY

Armand Eisen

ILLUSTRATED BY

Debbie Dieneman

LEOPARD

This edition published in 1995 by Leopard Books,
20 Vauxhall Bridge Road, London SW1V 2SA

First published in 1992 by Andrews and McMeel

ISBN 0 7529 0104 4

Design: Susan Hood and Mike Hortens
Art Direction: Armand Eisen, Mike Hortens and Julie Phillips
Art Production: Lynn Wine
Production: Julie Miller and Lisa Shadid

Classic Poems
for
Children

The Little Land

When at home alone I sit
And am very tired of it,
I have just to shut my eyes
To go sailing through the skies—
To go sailing far away
To the pleasant Land of Play;

To the fairy land afar
Where the Little People are;
Where the clover-tops are trees,
And the rain-pools are the seas,
And the leaves like little ships
Sail about on tiny trips.

—ROBERT LOUIS STEVENSON

7

There Was an Old Man

There was an Old Man with a beard,
Who said, "It is just as I feared!—
Two Owls and a Hen, four Larks and a Wren,
Have all built their nests in my beard!"

—EDWARD LEAR

The Owl

There was an old owl who lived in an oak;
The more he heard, the less he spoke.
The less he spoke, the more he heard.
Why aren't we like that wise old bird?

—ANONYMOUS

Did You Ever Go Fishing?

Did you ever go fishing on a bright sunny day—
Sit on a fence and have the fence give way?
Slide off the fence and rip your pants,
And see the little fishes
    do the hootchy-kootchy dance?

—ANONYMOUS

Ducks' Ditty

All along the backwater,
Through the rushes tall,
Ducks are a-dabbling,
Up tails all!
Ducks' tails, drakes' tails,
Yellow feet a-quiver,
Yellow bills all out of sight
Busy in the river!

—KENNETH GRAHAME

The Cow

The friendly cow all red and white,
I love with all my heart:
She gives me cream with all her might,
To eat with apple-tart.

—ROBERT LOUIS STEVENSON

If You See a Fairy Ring

If you see a fairy ring
    In a field of grass,
Very lightly step around,
    Tiptoe as you pass;
Last night fairies frolicked there,
    And they're sleeping somewhere near.

If you see a tiny fairy
    Lying fast asleep,
Shut your eyes and run away,
    Do not stay to peep;
And be sure you never tell,
    Or you'll break a fairy spell.

—ANONYMOUS

Time to Rise

A birdie with a yellow bill
Hopped upon the window-sill,
Cocked his shining eye and said:
"Ain't you 'shamed, you sleepy-head?"

—ROBERT LOUIS STEVENSON

Now the Day Is Over

Now the day is over,
Night is drawing nigh,
Shadows of the evening
Steal across the sky.

Now the darkness gathers,
Stars begin to peep,
Birds and beasts and flowers
Soon will be asleep.

—SABINE BARING-GOULD

My Shadow

—— ❦ ——

I have a little shadow
    that goes in and out with me,
And what can be the use of him
    is more than I can see.
He is very, very like me
    from the heels up to the head;
And I see him jump before me,
    when I jump into my bed.

—ROBERT LOUIS STEVENSON

15

Twinkle, Twinkle, Little Star

Twinkle, twinkle, little star,
How I wonder what you are!
Up above the world so high,
Like a diamond in the sky.
Twinkle, twinkle, little star,
How I wonder what you are!

—ANONYMOUS

I See the Moon

I see the moon,
And the moon sees me;
God bless the moon,
And God bless me.

—ANONYMOUS

17

A Child's Thought

At seven, when I go to bed,
I find such pictures in my head:
Castles with dragons prowling round,
Gardens where magic fruits are found;
Fair ladies prisoned in a tower,
Or lost in an enchanted bower;
While gallant horsemen ride by streams
That border all this land of dreams
I find, so clearly in my head
At seven, when I go to bed.

—ROBERT LOUIS STEVENSON

The Little Moon

———— ❧ ————

The night is come, but not too soon,
And sinking silently,
All silently, the little moon
Drops down behind the sky.

—HENRY WADSWORTH LONGFELLOW

The Firefly
Lights His Lamp

———— ❧ ————

Although the night is damp,
The little firefly ventures out,
And slowly lights his lamp.

—ANONYMOUS

What Is Pink?

What is pink? A rose is pink
    By the fountain's brink.
What is red? A poppy's red
    In its barley bed.
What is blue? The sky is blue
    Where the clouds float through.
What is white? A swan is white
    Sailing in the light.
What is yellow? Pears are yellow,
    Rich and ripe and mellow.
What is green? The grass is green,
    With small flowers between.
What is violet? Clouds are violet
    In the summer twilight.
What is orange? Why, an orange,
    Just an orange!

—CHRISTINA ROSSETTI

Pippa's Song

The year's at the spring,
And day's at the morn;
Morning's at seven;
The hill-side's dew-pearl'd;
The lark's on the wing;
The snail's on the thorn;
God's in His heaven—
All's right with the world!

—ROBERT BROWNING

Four Seasons

Spring is showery, flowery, bowery.
Summer: hoppy, choppy, poppy.
Autumn: wheezy, sneezy, freezy.
Winter: slippy, drippy, nippy.

—ANONYMOUS

22

Caterpillar

Brown and furry
Caterpillar in a hurry,
Take your walk
To the shady leaf, or stalk,
Or what not,
Which may be the chosen spot.
No toad spy you,
Hovering bird of prey pass by you;
Spin and die,
To live again a butterfly.

—CHRISTINA ROSSETTI

Who Has Seen the Wind?

Who has seen the wind?
Neither I nor you:
But when the leaves hang trembling,
The wind is passing through.

Who has seen the wind?
Neither you nor I:
But when the leaves bow down their heads,
The wind is passing by.

—CHRISTINA ROSSETTI

The Wind

I saw you toss the kites on high
And blow the birds about the sky;
And all around I heard you pass,
Like ladies' skirts across the grass—
  O wind, a-blowing all day long,
  O wind, that sings so loud a song!

—ROBERT LOUIS STEVENSON

Rain

The rain is raining all around,
It falls on field and tree,
It rains on the umbrellas here,
And on the ships at sea.

—ROBERT LOUIS STEVENSON

White Coral Bells

White coral bells upon
  a slender stalk.
Lilies of the valley
  deck my garden walk.
O don't you wish that you
  could hear them ring?
That can happen only
  when the fairies sing.

—ANONYMOUS

The Rainbow

There are bridges on the rivers,
As pretty as you please;
But the bow that bridges heaven,
And overtops the trees,
And builds a road from earth to sky,
Is prettier far than these.

—CHRISTINA ROSSETTI

Sweet and Low

Sweet and low, sweet and low,
  Wind of the western sea,
Low, low, breathe and blow,
  Wind of the western sea!

Over the rolling waters go,
Come from the dying moon, and blow,
  Blow him again to me;
While my little one,
    while my pretty one, sleeps.

—ALFRED, LORD TENNYSON

The Sea

——— ❦ ———

Behold the wonders of the mighty deep,
Where crabs and lobsters learn to creep,
And little fishes learn to swim,
And clumsy sailors tumble in.

—ANONYMOUS

At the Sea-side

——— ❦ ———

When I was down beside the sea
A wooden spade they gave to me
To dig the sandy shore.

My holes were empty like a cup.
In every hole the sea came up,
Till it could come no more.

—ROBERT LOUIS STEVENSON

Happy Thought

The world is so full of a number of things,
I'm sure we should all be as happy as kings.

—ROBERT LOUIS STEVENSON

The Swing

How do you like to go up in a swing,
Up in the air so blue?
Oh, I do think it the pleasantest thing
Ever a child can do!

—ROBERT LOUIS STEVENSON

Grasshoppers Three

Grasshoppers three a-fiddling went,
Hey, ho, never be still!
They paid no money toward their rent,
But all day long with elbow bent
They fiddled a tune called Rillaby-rill,
Fiddled a tune called Rillaby-ree.

—ANONYMOUS

Three Ghostesses

Three little ghostesses,
Sitting on postesses,
Eating buttered toastesses,
Greasing their fistesses,
Up to their wristesses,
Oh, what beastesses
To make such feastesses!

—ANONYMOUS

31

A Wee Little Worm

A wee little worm in a hickory-nut
Sang, happy as he could be,
"O I live in the heart
    of the whole round world,
    And it all belongs to me!"

—JAMES WHITCOMB RILEY

Hurt No Living Thing

Hurt no living thing;
Ladybird, nor butterfly,
Nor moth with dusty wing,
Nor cricket chirping cheerily,
Nor grasshopper so light of leap,
Nor dancing gnat, nor beetle fat,
Nor harmless worms that creep.

—CHRISTINA ROSSETTI